'WHEELS'

Camplejohn brothers at Darfield Main Wesley School, 1898.
Front row: 4th is Amos, 5th is Sidney, 7th is Walter. Second row: 7th is Colin.

'WHEELS'

THE EARLY LIFE OF
SIDNEY (JOHNNY) CAMPLEJOHN
OF DARFIELD

Born 10th March 1894 – Died 15th March 1989
Taken from an Autobiographical Manuscript hand-written by him in 1985

Darfield Area
Amenity Society Limited
2006

ISBN 0-901100-65-X

Designed and Printed by
NORTHEND CREATIVE PRINT SOLUTIONS
Clyde Road, Sheffield S8 0TZ
Tel: 250 0331 Fax: 250 0676
Email: ks@northend.co.uk

FOREWORD

When volunteers in Darfield Museum were collecting pictures and artefacts concerning the development of transport in Darfield, I was handed a number of foolscap sheets, hand-written by Sidney Camplejohn, and loaned by his son Dennis. Once I started reading through them that evening I could not stop until I had read them through completely. What a picture they presented! With the agreement of Dennis and the Camplejohn family, the sheets were typed into computer form by Aubrey Venables, Vice-Chairman of the Amenity Society, and they were then lightly edited for publication. Here is the result.

What a story!

Here the reader experiences life for a young teenager in the coal mines shortly after the turn of the 19th century; learns of the pitfalls of driving passenger transport in the days when licence, insurance or training were unnecessary, sees the maintenance of vehicles on a DIY basis; faces the practicalities, horrors and humour of life as an ambulance driver at the front in the First World War. And with the end of war and demobilisation, the written story finishes all too soon.

Sidney went on to develop their transport company in Darfield to include not only passenger transport but also heavy goods vehicles. During his life he made a valuable contribution to village life in countless ways. Darfield has much to thank and remember him for, and not least for taking the effort in his retirement to put these words down onto paper.

Geoffrey Hutchinson
Chairman, Darfield Area Amenity Society Limited.
February 2006

CHAPTER ONE

I, Sidney Camplejohn, was born at 59 Hope Street, Low Valley, Wombwell, Barnsley on 10th March 1894. In the year 1902 we moved into 128, Alderney Cottages, Darfield which is approximately 250 yards from where I was born, and lived in Darfield all my life except a period of almost four years in the Army during the 1914-1918 war. I am trying to go through the experiences of my life which has not been all easy going, and I was not brought up on what you would call 'silver spoon fed'.

At three years of age I can remember quite well going to school one Monday morning, my aunt taking me. There was another boy – Willie Page. He was taken by his elder sister. We were put in the hands of the Headmaster whose name was Mr. Timothy Harding. At that school I had three more brothers, older than myself, namely Colin, nine years, Walter seven and Amos five years. My father worked at Darfield Main Colliery as a surface worker, and the earnings at the Pit Top were very low.

My brother Amos and myself were usually together and later on one of our chief enjoyment was marbles. We usually finished the day with one of us having his trousers pockets bulging with marbles. The game that we usually played at school was what we called Chock. To make a chock, we used to scoop the ground at the bottom of a wall like a cup or a deep saucer, and two could play this game, but each player had to put in the same number of marbles. Two players would agree to a game and one would say to the other I'll set you four on between the two that would be eight marbles. One player would get the eight marbles in his hand and throw them in the Chock and if there were an even number in the chock the thrower would keep the eight marbles, therefore he would have won four marbles, then the other person would do the same and if it should be an odd number he would have lost eight marbles altogether. This used to be one of the popular games during playtime.

I don't remember many activities, except the Boer War which commenced approximately 1899 or 1900, and our most enjoyable time was either 1902 or 1903 when the war finished. I think we won that war as we used to get a number of the boys with tin cans or buckets and go through the streets in Low Valley, making as much noise as possible and singing or shouting "We're Soldiers of the Queen my lads" or "Up Majubu shooting Kruger" I think Kruger was the General of the Boers. Regarding the schooling part I think I got on very well. At 10 years of age I was in Standard 7, and finished school at 13. We never had any teaching at Maths. I did not know what it meant. I was most outstanding at mental arithmetic.

When I was about nine years of age my brother Amos and myself used to take a wheelbarrow to Darfield Main Tip where they used to bring the dirt out from the Colliery every morning with Horse and Cart to empty into the ponds which were previously clay pits where clay had been taken out for the brickmaking kilns. We usually got a barrow full of coal. We would then get a good wash and clean up and breakfast which was not bacon and eggs, but dripping with bread dipped in. We enjoyed it and we never went to school on an empty stomach.

One Good Friday morning at approximately 8.00am we were awakened and startled as we slept in the front bedroom of 128, Alderney Cottages, Snape Hill, Darfield. My brother Amos and myself looked out from the bedroom window and saw a contraption chugging away. We did not know anything about it and we had not seen anything like it. Two of my uncles Walter and Thomas Septimus Camplejohn had evidently purchased this vehicle which was an 18-seater called the New Arrol Johnston, made in Paisley, Scotland and delivered by an Irishman. We only knew him as Pat. This driver lived with us for about a week until my cousin J. W. Camplejohn got a little information and tuition.

In those days I don't think there were clutch stops fitted, and it was impossible to get it in first gear or reverse without a tremendous amount of grinding of gears. The first party that this vehicle, called a motor charabanc, took on an outing was the Darfield Church Bell Ringers who just went on around Bawtry, Blyth and Tickhill and the various churches bell ringing. This vehicle was the start of Camplejohn Brothers. My parents had no financial interest, but we always considered we were part and parcel of it. This vehicle had only two cylinders and about 18 horsepower, although at times going up hills I think some of the

The Arrol Johnston.

The Arrol Johnston with J. W. Camplejohn driving. Photograph taken outside Middlewood Hall Lodge.

horses were not very active. Every time that it was going on a journey, my brother Amos and myself one at each side as the Chara was reversing would grease the driving chains with a hand brush with oil as that was the only way that they would get lubricated and protected from wear.

My brother and myself used to polish the brasswork, trim the paraffin lamps, keep them topped up with paraffin and see that the lamp wick was not too short. Every Saturday evening we used to go taking the fares with the chara running between Darfield and Wombwell. Fare was two pence each way, of course that two pence was only one hundred and twentieth part of a pound note. There were 240 pence in the £1. That was before the paper money. £1 was one gold sovereign.

Every Monday morning at about 8.00am Amos and myself would take the wheelbarrow to Snape Hill Coop to get the supplies for our family. As my mother used to do all the bakery and cookery, there would be approximately 10 to feed. The grocery list would start as follows: 10 stone bag of flour, 20 pounds of moist sugar, 4 lbs of lard, 1 dozen boxes of matches (11/2d per dozen boxes), 4 or 5 lbs of currants and raisins, and various small items. Potatoes, vegetables and fruit would be obtained from the various greengrocers. Every Friday either Amos or myself would go to Wombwell Great Central Railway Station to get the fresh butter for our grandmother Camplejohn, which was sent from her old home by her brother and sister John and Jane Dawson at Kilpin, a farm near Howden. This butter was sent in a large basket. During warm weather they used to cover the butter well with rhubarb leaves, and we usually received it in good condition. It was our job to deliver it to various friends and relatives.

After the fruit season had finished coming from Kilpin, Howden, Amos and myself used to walk to Wombwell on the Friday evening or Saturday morning and purchase from a fruit shop, Richardson's, which was at the bottom of Hough Lane. We would purchase either one or two gross of oranges and sell them at the local football ground, at Low Valley (George Hotel Ground). We use to get them about two for a penny and sell them at one penny each. We used to make a few shillings between us, my grandmother Camplejohn used to advise us and I think she was very hardworking and her advice was very helpful. Our parents did not take any money that we made as they knew we should not throw it away.

CHAPTER TWO

At 13 years of age, my schooling days expired and that was the full period of my education. I think that I was well up to the average at the three 'Rs', reading, writing and arithmetic. Within a few days of leaving school, I got a job of work at Dearne Valley Colliery, Little Houghton, which is a walk of about three miles each way. If it isn't it seemed like it. The first job was picking out the dirt from the coal on the small or lump coal belts, six days per week. A week's earnings were three half crowns or 7/6d, which is 90 pence at 240 to the pound, or otherwise 90/240.

After about one year on the coal belts in what was called the screens I was moved on to what was called the Gantry, which involved starting at the weigh bridge where about 10 or 12 tubs of coal linked together as they were brought up from the pit which was not up a shaft, as it was a drift mine, and both the miners and the Pit Ponies, which were brought out after every working shift, walked down. My job was to call the numbers out, from an iron disc called a Mottie. Each miner who filled the tub with coal, which would on the average be about nine or ten hundredweight or half a ton, would have his name on the Mottie. In the Weigh Office there would be one representative of the miners and one representing the Colliery. The one for the miners at my time there was George Harry Hirst, who later became

A Mottie.

Member of Parliament representing Labour. The representative for the company was William Stables, whose parents kept the Rising Sun Inn in Snape Hill, Darfield.

After the tubs had been weighed and checked it was my job to take them along the Gantry to the Tippler, and it was a slight decline and we used steel lockers into the wheels to steady and eventually stop, approaching the Tippler. Each tub would be unlinked at the Tippler. The operator of the Tippler would pull a lever to tip each tub over which would go on to the Riddle or Shaker, and separate the lumps from the small, and go on to their respective belts for removing any dirt before getting into the railway wagons. At 15 years of age I very often

The Durham Churchill photographed outside Middlewood Hall Lodge.

The Durham Churchill photographed in 1912 at Matlock Bath with a party of Mitchell's Main Colliery Deputies and Officials. The driver is Sidney Camplejohn.

Colin Camplejohn driving the Durham Churchill in Worksop 1912.

suffered with some internal trouble which was on the left hand side of my body. My father used to say 'you'll work it off, it's only a bit of belly ache', but I knew this feeling was not just belly ache.

About 1908, Camplejohn Brothers purchased a new motor charabanc, a 24-seater. The chassis was a Durham-Churchill built in Sheffield and the coachwork, or body, was made at Wilson Coachbuilders, Sheffield. This vehicle had a 35-horsepower Aster engine and this chara did a tremendous amount of running and it was very reliable for a few years after the 1914-18 war. This was also a chain drive vehicle, but the driving chains were not the roller type, but silent, similar to the timing chains at that time used on engines of most makes.

About 1909 we purchased an 18-seater second-hand Dennis from someone called Fox. I don't know why he was disposing of it. I think he was a Publican, probably could not make it pay. I started driving this chara when I was 17 years of age. The engine in this vehicle was a 4-cylinder French Aster and the cylinders four separate blocks. It had only three forward gears. Sometimes it was a difficult job and we were very pleased that it usually made it.

About 1909 there was a fire at Barnsley at a garage owned by a Publican, I think his name was Burrows. He kept the Union Inn and he owned two charas, one a Commer and one a

Billy Camplejohn, driver of the restored Dennis.
(Billy was later proprietor of 2 Vicar Road – now Darfield Museum)

The restored Dennis with a party of local Buffs outside the Sportsman Inn in Low Valley, Darfield.
Amos Camplejohn is driving.

Dennis. We purchased the Dennis remains of the chassis. I could not say how much our firm paid for the remains, but it would not be much. It was brought from Barnsley to our garage at Snape Hill by one of my mother's brothers, Mr. A. Ward who was a fruiterer and he brought it on his horse-drawn dray. I had not mentioned earlier that another uncle, James Camplejohn, was the Chief Engineer at Darfield Main Colliery. He and his son, William Camplejohn, both had a very good mechanical knowledge, and played a big part in repairing and erecting or assembling engines or transmissions of motor vehicles. Owing to the Dennis chassis going through a tremendous heat with the fire, the chassis frame was slightly out of shape, and we straightened it with large clamps after the frame had been heated by blow lamps, as we had no other methods in those days. When we finished the straightening up work, we slung from the roof rope blocks and lifted the complete chassis. Our garage had a loft at the front end, used for repairs. The front of the chassis including the engine was put through into the loft, the rear part of the chassis was carried by two large steel hangers from the roof, and long planks of timber which carried the weight of the rear end of the chassis. This garage had no electric lights at that time, although we had gas over the work bench in the loft.

My cousin, Willie Camplejohn, used to come early every evening as he was the mechanic and I was with him all the time. The lighting that we used was from a large accumulator which is now called a battery. This was charged up in the daytime. The engine was thoroughly overhauled and we replaced the old rear axle and fitted a new later type rear axle from Dennis Brothers Ltd., Guildford, which was what was called Worm Drive. Dennis Brothers were the first makers of that kind of driving axle. Eventually we got the chassis completed. Then we took the chassis to a firm called Stagg and Robson at Selby, Coach Builders, and they fitted an 18-seater chara body, complete with hood and all fittings.

We started running this chara and it broke the transmission shaft, which we had to get welded. We decided to remove the interior of the rear axle including the worm wheel which was brass and the worm shaft which was steel, case hardened. On checking the shaft we discovered it was slightly bent or out of line. We notified Dennis Brothers, and they sent us a new worm shaft. Then we had no more trouble.

This vehicle usually went on most of the hilly districts in Derbyshire – Matlock, Buxton, Dovedale, and it was one of the most reliable passenger vehicles we ever had. The engine was a White and Poppe 28-horsepower and it was very quiet and went up all hills with ease. At that time Dennis Brothers used all the engines they produced. They had the sole rights and no other passenger vehicle manufacturers could fit one in any new chassis. In later years Dennis Brothers took over the White and Poppe Engineering concern, and in the later war of 1914 to 1918, all Dennis lorries were completed by those engines.

I mentioned earlier Willie Camplejohn who was the main mechanic at our garage in the evenings, he also worked in the fitting shops at Darfield Main, but mostly at the garage and the pit, where he repaired and serviced the cars for the proprietors, who at that time were the only officials that had cars, namely Mr. T. W. H. Mitchell, who resided at Sandygate, Wath-on-Dearne, and Joseph Mitchell of Netherwood Hall, which was situated between Darfield Main Colliery and Mitchells Main Colliery. They were the owners of the two collieries. My uncle, T. S. Camplejohn, had a shop in Snape Hill which was a Beer off-Licence and General Groceries. Also, one room at the shop was set out as a bicycle shop which was owned by himself and his brother, W. Camplejohn. They also had a bicycle workshop at the rear.

They were agents for the cycle manufacturers New Hudson and Rover, and later Rudge Whitworth. I used to spend a lot of my time assisting in the cycle shop shed. I got used to building wheels up. We used to get the spokes and cut them to the exact length, then put them into the machine which you turned by hand which made the threads the exact size for the round headed nuts or nipples which went on the outside of the rim of the wheel. The rim had to have the same amount of holes as the hub. It took a while to learn. When the wheel was put together and complete, the wheel would be put into the trueing machine and it would be necessary to keep easing some of the nipples and tightening others while you got it true all round. Then you would check over to find if any of the spokes had gone too far through the nipples. If so, we should cut the ends or file them. When all was correct a fabric tape about ¾" wide would be wrapped round inside the rim, then the inner tube and tyre could be fitted. I found this work very interesting, but it took time. I don't think I should have made a big wage in building cycle wheels.

In the year 1909, owing to working out in the open at Dearne Valley Colliery and having a continuous attack of pains in the left side of my tummy, which was years later found to be a faulty left kidney, I then went to Darfield Main Colliery which is only about 250 yards away from my home and where there was more protection from the wintry weather.

My first job there was preparing the railway wagons for filling with large and small coal. My brother Amos was also on the coal belts. Before the wagons were put under the belts for filling, it was necessary to look inside to see if anything was inside, and that the bottom trap doors were properly closed and secure. One morning my brother Amos found a small metal like box. We did not know what it was, so my brother got a steel bar that we used when closing the bottom wagon door. It had a chisel shaped end. He put this box on a steel flat sheet and bashed away to open it, but before it opened out, there was such a bang, that it nearly deafened us, and it was heard all over the Pit Top. We were all really frightened. It was a Fog Signal. Someone must have thrown it in the empty wagon.

Occasionally my uncle, the chief engineer at the pit, would instruct me to have two or three days at Mr. J. Mitchell's of Netherwood Hall, to assist the gardener there. My job was to lead the pony pulling the horse-drawn lawn mower. That was a nice steady job. I would then go back to the wagons.

There was a period each working day, except Saturday, when the screens would be standing idle between 1.00pm and 2.00pm as the winding engines were carrying the afternoon shift workers down the pit and bringing up the morning shift. We called that Men Riding Time. This period was used for various activities for the boys, on various occasions mischievous. During the summer period a number of us would go to the river or dyke near Tiger Row. It was deep enough to swim in. One particular afternoon there was a gang of the boys bathing in the river, including two of my brothers, Walter and Amos. Walter was a reasonably good swimmer, and Amos was just on the point of learning. This particular day, I sat on the bank watching. One part of the river was rather deep, and Amos had done about two strokes and then must have been standing up to get his breath, and he was out of his depth, and I saw immediately that he was drowning. I shouted out to Walter, "Get Amos out he's drowning." Walter turned round and pulled him away. He didn't say thanks Walt, but he remarked, "It's ta'en thee some b——- time lad."

At 16 years of age, my uncle Jim sent me to work in the Blacksmith's Shop as a striker to the foreman blacksmith Mr. W. Gibbs. He was an expert Rope Splicer. He could also splice cotton ropes, which were used as well as steel ropes. Whenever he had to go down the pit for rope repairs, I went with him and it was very interesting work. When I first went into the Blacksmith's Shop to work I never realised that they had such various kinds of jobs, but the blacksmiths in those days were marvellous craftsmen, and it was far from easy work. Each blacksmith had a hearth which burnt small coke and compressed air for getting the various amount of heat required for welding etc. W. Gibbs and Joe Turner had their hearths very near to each other. There was another blacksmith's hearth at the other end of the shop, which would be approximately 9 or 10 yards away. The Steam Hammer was also very near to W. Gibbs and Joe Turner.

I realised later on one or two large and difficult jobs that were undertaken. One was a very large steel shaft which had broken into two parts. I believe it was from the screens. This was the time that the two blacksmiths had to work together. One blacksmith would get one part of the broken shaft and check up with each end, and if there were any shaped ends or bolt or pin holes, they would have to be in line. They would sometimes lay it out on the floor of the shop and get the exact length. After checking, the two blacksmiths would get one each of the broken shafts, get them in each fire and when they got their pieces of steel shafts white hot they would hammer them out and taper to the right shape for joining together. Then they would both put their pieces into the fire and get them white hot. They would time it so that both would be sending sparks out at the same time. The two strikers would have their striking hammer ready and standing each side of the anvil. It had to be accurate timing. One blacksmith would put his part quickly endways on the anvil and the other would lay his on the top, then the strikers would start with their large striking hammers bashing away as quickly as possible. The blacksmith would keep turning it and pointing with his hand hammer. Sometimes it had to be heated up again to get more hammering. When it was welded up, it would be brought to the steam hammer.

If it was a round shaft, after coming from the steam hammer, we should get a steel block which would fit into the square hole in the anvil. The block would be shaped on the top, shaped half round the same dimensions for the welded part of the shaft to lay on. There would also be a block that the blacksmith could hold on top with a handle of steel. The striker would hammer at this block. Of course the section of the shaft would have to be kept heated. Sometimes after a job of this kind, the shaft may have to go into the Fitting Shop to be put into a large lathe to be checked for alignment and accuracy. Occasionally when we had cleared all the emergency work Mr. Gibbs would decide to make a few Collier's Wedges as these were the most important tool that the colliers used in those days, and the colliers very often used to come into the blacksmith's shop to see if Mr. Gibbs could fix them up with one or two wedges. He usually had a few in readiness. These wedges were forged out of old corve axles after the wheels had been knocked off. These axles were about three feet long and two inches thick round. The wedges were about eight or nine inches long. The shape of the wedge approximately when flattened to shape was about three inches wide and approximately one and a half inches deep, and gradually tapered. To finish the wedge off the blacksmith would get a strip of special steel, what was called Double Shear Steel, get it into the fire and get them both to welding heat. He would cut the end off so that the hardening steel would be left on the end of the wedge. When all was completed the blacksmith would then get the wedge to a dull red heat, rub it with sandstone and dip in water, and watch it carefully and eventually a blue shade would come down the point of the wedge. He would quickly dip it into the water trough. That would be the completion of the wedge.

My blacksmith would never take any cash. I used to be amused. The colliers would come into the shop and say, "Have you got a wedge Bill?" Bill would say, "Aye, ah think I've got one or two." My blacksmith, Bill, was a pipe smoker and most of the colliers not being allowed matches or cigarettes down the pit they mostly had Ogdens, thick or thin Twist Tobacco. This they chewed down the pit and Bill always had two tobacco tins in his pocket. He always pulled out the empty tin. The colliers would see his baccy tin was empty and would say immediately, "Have some of mine Bill." The price of tobacco in those days was about 1½d. or three half pence for an ounce. Woodbine cigarettes were five for a penny, Gold Flake three pence for a packet of 10. 240 pence to £1 or gold sovereign. I don't think my blacksmith would spend much in tobacco.

We commenced work at 6.00am every morning. The first job was to get the fire going and it would usually be about 6.30am before we got going with the usual work. I remember one morning, my uncle came in at 6.00am to give W. Gibbs particulars to forge something that had broken or worn in the screens. He drew the sketch and measurements on the steel cover of the hearth with white chalk and then sat down on a large wooden tool box. While he was still there, we had to keep busy making something. I remarked to my uncle still sitting on the box and said, "You know that box is very damp on the top. You will be getting rheumatics." He quickly replied, "You young devil, you want to get rid of me." Of course he was right. The blacksmith had a good laugh.

Throughout the period that I was working in the Blacksmith's Shop, I was, along with my father and Amos, my brother, dressing bricks. Camplejohn Brothers had purchased a portion of land and a section of the Brick Buildings from the claypit which was previously owned by the Mitchell Brothers Colliery owners. The bricks we were dressing were used in the erection of the first part of Camplejohn Brothers Pitt Street Garage. When I reached the age of 17 years, that would be 1911, I left Darfield Main Colliery to start driving motor charabancs.

CHAPTER THREE

My first driving was on an 18-seater Dennis. This was a vehicle which Camps purchased from the previous owner called Fox of Barnsley. I remember quite well the first party I took out was to South Owram and Halifax. I don't know if I went off my route a little, but I recollect going up a rather steep hill and the road was very narrow. I was in low gear. It was on a Sunday morning. Coming down the hill was a Parson, on a pedal cycle. He would be going to a morning service at some local church or chapel. He seemed to be surprised at seeing a motor charabanc going up the hill and as I was going past, he turned his head aside and in doing so, he fell off his cycle. I dare not stop, as I should not have been able to start again. I hope he did not include that incident in his sermon. When I got to the top of this hill, we had a few minutes rest. We could see Halifax very much lower than we were. Anyhow, we completed the journey and got home alright.

During this period, we used to take miners from Wombwell, Darfield, Low Valley, also Broomhill, to Houghton Main Colliery with two charas in the morning, afternoon and evening shifts. About 1910 or 1911 a new housing estate was built at Woodlands, Brodsworth near to the colliery. It was called a Model Village and housed practically all miners from various parts of the country. Doncaster was the nearest town which was approximately four miles away. The only way the people could get to Doncaster was by walking about 1½ miles to Adwick-le-Street station and go by train. We started about 1911 sending a chara to start running from Woodlands to Doncaster. We had not a regular timetable, but in the week it was a steady job. On Saturdays we used to send an extra chara. There were one or two other operators used to come on Saturdays.

About 1910 or 1911, Camplejohn Brothers built a new cinema called the Empire at Adwick-le-Street. My father, I believe, was the largest shareholder in this enterprise. The authorities of that area had planned to build a large estate at Adwick-le-Street but unfortunately they had come to the conclusion that the land was too low, and subject to flooding, so the new estate was built at Carcroft, near to the colliery. Therefore this was a disappointing set back to the Picture Palace Enterprise. We eventually got everything going. Sometimes it did reasonably.

Of course in those days they were silent films and the talking films came a few years later, and these films were controlled in this country by an American concern called the Western Electric. When a very prominent or exciting film was in circulation, all the picture houses in the large cities got the first chance of obtaining them. Months after if a small cinema proprietor got the chance of showing one it was almost like bribery. They had to agree to take probably two or three films of rubbish. Therefore you would get a reasonable week with the special film, then two or three weeks of small attendances and probably a good number of them disappointed with the films. Camplejohn brothers were operating this cinema throughout the 1914-1918 war. Eventually we sold it. I can definitely say we did not make a fortune out of it, but I don't think we lost much, but there were some very difficult periods. I put about £50 into the venture and I think I received about the same amount back. End of cinema.

Coming back to the passenger side of the business, I occasionally took a load of miners on the morning shift and brought a load of night shift workers back to Darfield and Wombwell, then got a good breakfast and off to Woodlands and do about five or six journeys to Doncaster. We used to park the chara in Trafford Street, Doncaster during lunch time about 12.30pm to 1.30pm and we had arrangements at the Albany Restaurant which was near the market, and there were usually a load of passengers when we came back to the vehicle. The driver in the week days could manage to take the fares without any difficulty.

We had one young man who was friendly with my brother Amos, and he had been a good local boxer and he was strong and fit. He sometimes did a bit of conducting, but on Saturday nights he would see the charas safely away, as there were a number of them had been over drinking, and they often tried to get on to the running boards on the offside of the chara. This man of ours whose name was Mick Philbin, an Irish lad, used to pull them off and shout to the driver to carry on. He got into a few scrapes, but he always came out alright. I remember one funny incident when Mick was taking fares on my chara. He was collecting at the rear end and one particular man had probably had too much to drink and was refusing to pay his fare, and there was a bit of an argument. A lady passenger sitting near remarked to the man "Hey thee, pay thi' fare; my lodger's been in bed a fortnight through that bloke hitting him!" Mick got his fare.

Some time about 1912 we were still running on paraffin side and tail lamps, and acetylene headlamps – nothing electrical whatever; no self starter, only starting handle, and magneto, which made the spark to the sparking plugs. You could get a shock if you touched the plug top or the wire that was the electric connection to the magneto. We did occasionally have a 9-volt accumulator or battery as they are called now, and rig two light bulbs inside when the hood was in covered position. We used to have much difficulty in keeping the rear lamp alight, and some of the Police were very keen to prosecute and get an easy case without any opposition. I was summonsed on numerous occasions.

I remember quite well a ginger haired bobby once stopped me and took particulars. I appeared at Doncaster Police Court and the fine was 19 shillings or 21 days down the line. The same policeman took the 19 shillings from me after the case, and remarked, "What about a drink for me?" I replied without hesitation, "Oh yes, you can have a drink but you take it out of the nineteen bob I have just given you." The year would be about 1912 or 1913.

I used to enjoy running on the Woodlands to Doncaster run except practically every Saturday evening I used to have a very sickly and heavy feeling on the left side of my body. When I used to get home approaching midnight, as soon as I entered my home my mother knew. She would remark, "Oh dear, lad, tha's got that awful complaint again." I did not want any supper. I should go to bed and have about four or five hours agonising pains and getting in and out of bed vomiting. I always knew when the attack was coming to an end there would be a kind of acidy taste in my throat and I should know that was the end of it, and I should fall off to sleep and get up at the usual time and enjoy a good breakfast. I should be alright again for another week or two. It was my left kidney that was faulty.

Doncaster was recognised as an important cattle market, and it was a very busy time on Saturday. When farmers or butchers purchased cattle they may have to be taken anything from five to 20 miles by road to their destination of the purchaser. There were no motor road transport carriers in those days, but there were always a number of men available called Drovers. A purchaser would hire one of these men to take the cows to his farm or premises. The cattle would eventually go from one side of the road to the other especially if there was a nice grass verge where they could get something to chew. I think that was what happened one Saturday evening. I think it was 1913.

I had got a load of passengers at Woodlands and going along what was called Park Side going in the direction of Highfield and Doncaster, when one of the cows came from one side and walked right into the front of my chara. It knocked the cow down and the front end of my vehicle went over the top. I got all the passengers out and we managed to drag the animal out which was dead. Fortunately, I had kept the engine running, and I got all the passengers to Doncaster. I then had a look round the vehicle to see what damage had been done, and saw the starting handle had been knocked back, and I should not be able to use that and also the radiator was damaged and leaking. I got a young lad at Doncaster end with an empty two gallon petrol can to get it filled with water each time I arrived at the Doncaster end, and also another at Woodlands. I managed to keep the vehicle going and complete the journeys. I considered if we were unlucky and had to pay for the cost of the cow, we had better take a bit of cash towards it.

My conductor at this time was my cousin, Herbert Camplejohn. He would be about 15 years of age. He was on the running boards on the near side of the vehicle taking the fares at the time of the accident. A few weeks later the farmer who owned the cow that was run over and killed, sued Camplejohn Brothers for the cost of the cow and expenses etc. We appeared at the County Court at Doncaster. I took along my cousin Herbert who was conducting on the chara. I don't remember who, but the farmer had a prosecuting Solicitor from Doncaster. I believe his name was Marshall. He was a very dominant and aggressive person. I should imagine he would frighten a lot of witnesses with that attitude.

I was called into the witness box and the Solicitor started banging questions and I did not let him bully me. I was careful in replying. He kept suggesting various items and then in an excitable manner he said, "I suggest you lost your head." I remarked in a slow Yorkshire reply, "Well, it's on yet." We won the case. The Magistrates came to the conclusion that the cattle were not under proper control.

My brother Amos was at the same Court, same day, for injuring a horse whilst driving a chara. The horse was being broken in for the road and it had not got used to vehicles and the normal everyday road users. Result – unfortunately he lost his case.

About this period, 1912, Barnsley Football Club was having a very good run in the Cup. At that time it was called the English Cup. In the sixth round that year, they played Bradford City four times. Then Barnsley eventually won the Round which put them into the Semi Final with Swindon Town at Nottingham. We went to this match with a chara as we had been to all the previous matches, (Barnsley won), and met West Bromwich Albion in the Final, which was then played at Crystal Palace Ground, London. That was the only match I did not see. Fortunately it was a drawn game and the replay was at Bramall Lane, Sheffield United's ground. Barnsley won the Cup. I saw that match. The Barnsley player that scored the winning goal was Harry Tufnell. That was the only time the Cup has been won in Yorkshire on a Yorkshire ground.

We were still operating all our passenger vehicles with magnetos, which were mostly Bosch of German manufacture, and they were very good and reliable. I remember one particular journey, I was taking a party to Matlock and Buxton, and proceeding along the Abbeydale Road, Sheffield, towards Baslow. The engine stopped and I came to the conclusion it was the magneto. I got one of my passengers to turn the starting handle slowly to watch the contact breaker going round and realised that the contact spring had broken, and the rocker arms were in the open position all the time. These contacts had a small portion of platinum soldered on where they made the spark to the plugs. I felt very worried. I studied the working of the contacts and came to the conclusion, if I got a small piece of rubber about twice the thickness of an ordinary match stick and wedged it between the rocker arm and the rocker housing, the cam section of the rocker arm would open the points and the rubber wedged in this position would close them. So I got my pocket knife out and cut a small piece of rubber from one of the rear solid tyres and wedged it in to the contact breaker, got the engine started up and everything went perfectly. I don't think that we were held up more than approximately 40 minutes. Later I found out that the rubber rings inside the mineral water bottles were ideal for a make do and mend, as they were of softer rubber and more pliable.

About 1913, probably September, the Hickleton Main Colliery had their annual day outing to Blackpool by train from Frickley Railway Station and we took two charas. My brother Amos and myself had delivered one load of passengers and went back to Thurnscoe for a second load, and we managed to put all the remaining passengers on to Amos's chara, so I said, "I will take my chara to the bottom of Clayton Lane, Thurnscoe and then go along with him to collect his fares." On the return journey from Frickley, we saw another motor charabanc which was owned by two partners from Darfield, namely Storey and Wood. This vehicle was of French manufacture and not a suitable vehicle for two new starters. Evidently this vehicle had taken one load of passengers with Mr. Storey, and when he had dropped them off at Frickley Station, he went on the trip to Blackpool by train and left his partner Mr. Wood to take the unladen chara back to Darfield. Unfortunately, he could not keep the vehicle on the road. My brother and myself got it back on the road and he requested me to drive this vehicle to the bottom of Clayton Lane, which I did. I believe he got ditched again before he got to Darfield. Later I told both Storey and Wood that this vehicle was not in a fit condition to carry passengers. They had purchased this vehicle from Reginald Lambert whose garage was at Waterdale, Doncaster.

Later Storey and Wood were suing Mr. Lambert for selling them a vehicle that was not in a roadworthy condition. I was summonsed to go to the Court at Doncaster as chief witness. Reg Lambert who sold this vehicle was the son of Mr. Lambert, Chemist in Wombwell High Street, and I believe it was Lambert's Solicitor who named me as a witness. I felt in an uncomfortable position as I knew both sides, but I could not say anything good about this vehicle. I said in the witness box that I only drove this vehicle approximately 1½ miles and I had difficulty in keeping it on the road, and I would not have liked to have driven it far myself. Mr. Lambert was trying to point out the various points saying there were ball bearings in various parts. The magistrate remarked, "It sounds as if it is made of ball bearings." Result, Storey and Wood won this case and I believe they got their payment refunded, and I do not remember Storey and Wood doing any more activities in passenger transport.

I am just trying to remember the various people around Darfield, Low Valley and Wombwell who were passenger vehicle operators. Here are a few: T. Lee and Son, Wombwell; T. Burrows and Son; Horace Laycock; Charlie Darlow; Long & Burgin; Blackburn; J. Hunsley; Mellor; Walter Bird; W. Pickerill and Son; W. Hardman; Lindley and Spencer; Greenhow Brothers; Dan Smith; Martin Stenton; Button; Parry & Shreeves; Leeson and Brown; Baldwin Latham. In those days there were no restrictions, no Road Fund Licence and the insurance was not compulsory and some of the above would fix about eight or nine temporary seats into a Ford T-Type van, and carry people to Barnsley or Doncaster.

It was about 1913, I took a party of approximately 24 passengers to Scarborough with the Churchill chara and my brother Walter went along with me for a day out. He sat on my right hand side. On the return journey, a very unfortunate accident occurred. One of my acetylene headlamps had gone out and I asked my brother Walter to get out and put a match to light it. We were just approaching Woodlands, as I was pulling up my brother opened the side door and got out before I had completely stopped and fell on his head. Fortunately this accident occurred very near to Bickerstaffs shop at Woodlands and we were very friendly with the elderly lady and her daughter, as we occasionally went in there for a meal whilst on service. However they kindly fixed him up with a bed for the night and we got him home the next morning. I think he had a slight concussion and it was not as serious as we thought.

We were still running daily services from Woodlands to Doncaster. I remember one Saturday I had completed a full day and returning with the empty chara except for my conductor, and the offside front wheel came off. In those days the front axle ends comprised of a brass thrust collar, a brass cylindrical bush, a brass washer and a steel washer. The shaft end was very fine threads with a split pin, and with the vibration and solid rubber tyres the threads on the axle used to get stripped, and this particular Saturday night the offside wheel came off. I fixed it up to get home.

As this vehicle was booked for a journey early on Sunday morning to take a party for a military event at York which was described as York Military Sunday, I decided to notify my uncle. He was the Chief Engineer at Darfield Main Colliery and he came along with his son and trimmed the axle end and re-screwed it with Whitworth Thread and fitted a new Whitworth nut and made it secure. The vehicle was all ready next morning and I went to York without any more trouble. After putting the vehicle into the garage, whilst I was getting my supper, my uncle came into the house and he remarked, "Well lad, how many wheels have you come home on tonight?" I replied, "Five with what I had in my hands!" He threatened me in a joking way.

In 1914, we were still running from Woodlands to Doncaster and I believe it was during that year that the Government was gradually using paper ten shilling and one pound notes, and we did not like accepting the paper money, but we had no alternative. During the weekdays I used to go running the service without a conductor, and when I collected a gold coin, I used to put the half sovereigns in my left side waistcoat pocket and the sovereigns in the right because it would be difficult if you mixed them with the silver, as a sixpence was the same size as a half sovereign, and a shilling equalled in size one sovereign. (A bucket full of those would be very useful today!)

During this period, I don't think they had any garages with the pumps to supply petrol. We had to purchase it in two gallon cans and the main suppliers were Shell, also Pratts. Mitchell Main and Houghton Main Chemical Works were in production with Benzol and we used to take one of the charas and load up with approximately 150 two gallon cans, that would be 300 gallons. The petrol tanks on the vehicles were under the front seat, which extended to approximately the width of the body and the fuel to the carburettor was gravity fed, no fuel pump. I have known on a few occasions, when the petrol tank has been getting low and had to go up a very steep hill, then the carburettor would be higher than the fuel in the tank. There was no other alternative but to do a few shunts to get the vehicle round and go up the hill in reverse gear.

During this period the price of petrol was approximately eight pence per gallon and Benzol about the same. 30 gallons for £1.00, 240 pence in the pound. Early 1914, Camplejohn Brothers purchased a new 28-seater Dennis charabanc. This vehicle was built completely by Dennis Brothers of Guildford. One of my elder brothers or my cousin mostly drove it. I took it out a few times and it went very smoothly and was a treat to drive. Unfortunately there were very dark clouds over the country as the Kaiser, who was the

Emperor of Germany, made war on France. England, or Great Britain, went to war to assist France. That was the start of the 1914-1918 war.

The war started August 1914 and we were still running the passenger vehicles on the Woodlands to Doncaster and Darfield and Wombwell to Barnsley, also the miners to Houghton Main Colliery. There were a lot of the Regular Army and Territorial Soldiers going over to France, but everything seemed to be running normally, shops and various businesses including coal mines. I was still going down to Woodlands and one particular Saturday evening, I was bringing a load of passengers with the chara from Doncaster on the Great North Road. Approximately 200 yards from the Sun Inn the rear nearside axle end broke which was a solid axle, being a chain drive vehicle. Fortunately we had a very strong trolley at the garage that we used to move very bulky and heavy parts. This trolley had two very strong steel wheels on a heavy duty axle shaft. There was a wooden kind of platform, and a long wooden shaft with a short iron tube at the end for pushing or pulling.

We got this trolley underneath the near side rear spring, then let the weight down on to the trolley. The long wooden shaft of the trolley was in line with the underneath of the chassis frame. We used some very strong rope and wrapped it round the chassis frame and the wooden shaft of the trolley. We put on two of these rope fastenings, then to make them secure we made a loop so that we could put a steel bar through and make what we call a 'twitch'. The bar was put through the loop in the rope and twisted. When tight the bar was fitted into the chassis frame which was U-shape, and made secure so that it could not work out. One of our other charas which had been running the service came along with a towing bar and towed me home to Darfield which was a distance of 10 miles. We did not go above seven or eight miles per hour. We got it to our garage without any more trouble. A new axle shaft was put on on the Monday.

Occasionally when I was not running the Woodlands run I should be taking private parties to the seaside or Derbyshire district. One particular party I took to Castleton and Buxton and on the return journey was getting through Sheffield at approximately 9.30pm. Proceeding down the hill from Pitsmoor, the Main Barnsley Road, had a double line tram track. About half way down this hill there was a kind of a farm land on my left side, and unfortunately three or four cows had broken out of the field and ran right into the main road, across the front of my chara. Two of these cows were pushed forward two or three yards, not run over this time. They got away and someone must have got them back into the field. We were really very lucky being on the tram route.

I got all the passengers out, which was a Ladies Party, and got them on to the first tram going into Sheffield and they got the last train from Sheffield to Darfield. After getting all the passengers fixed up for home, I then reversed the chara on to the farm lane. I had a good look round the front end of the chara. I knew the radiator was badly damaged, and all the water lost out, but I could not find any other damage. My next job was one night sleeping in the chara. I'm afraid I did not sleep very well, I kept hearing some of the cows mooing and in the early hours, I kept waking up cold. However I got through the night eventually.

Whilst I was trying to get warm outside I had a very pleasant surprise. A young lady came out from one of the residential houses with my breakfast on a tray. I do not know if she was a servant or mistress of the house, but it was very kind of them. I told her how much I appreciated it and thanked her. Shortly after, my eldest brother Colin and one of my uncles came with another chara in case the vehicle had to be towed home. They also brought about two dozen vent pegs. These are wooden rounds tapered to a point. Publicans use them for letting air into wooden beer barrels. They also brought a sharpened flat chisel similar to a wood chisel and they found approximately 12 radiator tubes were fractured. They cut with the chisel top and bottom and knocked a vent peg into the holes where the broken tubes had been. We then filled the radiator with water and drove the chara home without any leakage. I believe we ran the vehicle for a week or two. Later the radiator was removed and top and bottom removed, the broken ends which were on the bottom and top of the radiator had to be removed by heating and melting the soldering in order for fitting new tubes which would need soldering.

A little while later, the last new passenger vehicle that we purchased was commandeered by the military authorities. The passenger body had to be removed and the chassis taken to a military depot down south to be fitted up with a lorry body for military use. The passenger body was raised from the ground level and rested on two long planks laid on top of empty oil barrels at the front end of our garage in Snape Hill Road, Darfield. A new chassis was ordered from Dennis Brothers of Guildford, Surrey, to be allocated to Camplejohn Brothers as soon as possible after the end of the war. That passenger body was stored in that place under cover until 1921.

The body built in 1913 that was put into store after the chassis was commandeered for military purposes.

CHAPTER FOUR

We were still operating the other vehicles and a lot of the young men were joining the Forces. An Army Officer came to our home and told my mother that the Army was wanting experienced heavy vehicle motor drivers to join the Mechanical Transport of the Army Service Corps. My brother Amos and myself decided that we would join up. We went to Sheffield and had a medical test and passed A1. We were detailed to report at Grove Park, London on a certain Monday and given a railway warrant or pass to get there. We were both working as normal the last few days. The last journey I did was with a party from the Red Lion Inn at Braithwell near Maltby, Rotherham. I took them to Hull and Beverley. I believe they went through a brewery. On the return journey I pulled in at the New Inn at Holme on Spalding Moor, and whilst there, I remember quite well re-charging the Carbide Generator which I had fitted on the offside running board. This was used to supply the acetylene gas to the head lamps – no electricity. I completed my last journey and dropped this party off at the Red Lion Inn, Braithwell, at midnight Sunday and got home about 1.00am Monday morning. I was on the train, which is approximately one mile to Wombwell Main Station, at 8.00am, which we walked along with my brother Amos, W. Page, J. Woollin and Len Pendlebury, as all the five of us had joined up together.

The route was Wombwell to Sheffield Midland Station, to St. Pancras, London, then Waterloo to Grove Park. I can't say it was what you would call a happy and jovial journey although some of them were playing cards etc. I remember remarking to them, "I wonder how we shall find our way to Grove Park, when we get to the Station?" as it was dark. But before the train had stopped, there were the Army Sergeants, bawling out, "Fall in, two deep, you're in the Army now." They marched us to what was termed the Barracks about half a mile away. When we arrived, a roll call and checking up, we were issued with a blanket each and we had to sleep on the concrete floor and landings at this place, which I think had previously been a work house. My brother Amos and myself used one blanket to lay on, the other on top. That was our last time we had together.

When we were on the point of getting to sleep, a Sergeant came along and shouted out "Have you all got two blankets?" One chap replied "Yes, I've got two." The Sergeant bawled out, "Give me one of the buggers; you're only entitled to one!"

Anyhow, we got over the first night, far from comfortable. I believe the first breakfast was about 8.30am, but before we had breakfast we were wakened up to get washed, shaved etc., (cold water), and then a roll call to make sure no one was missing, and then breakfast. After breakfast they kept having roll calls and picking a certain number out for various jobs. My brother Amos was one of the first to go to test for driving. He got through alright and got his khaki uniform either the second or third day. I was detailed along with some more recruits to be tested on light cars. I passed through on a Sunbeam light car. Whilst I was lined up for my uniform I heard a Sergeant calling out names from the other side of a fence and heard him shout 'Camplejohn' distinctly. Within a couple of minutes, those from the other side of the fence were marching past, including Amos. He spotted me as he was passing and shouted, "Goodbye Johnny." That was the last time I saw him, as he went to Egypt and later to Salonika. It was a long goodbye. Never saw him again until well after the war finished.

I myself was still at Grove Park. Some had uniform and some still in civilian clothes. The Sergeants were continually calling them on Parade, and sometimes asking for volunteers for various duties. On one occasion he shouted out, "Fall out all the Rolls-Royce Drivers." He got about nine or 10 of them, some of them in their chauffeur's uniform with leggings etc. Later on I saw them walking through the Parade Ground with five gallon oil drums, which were used in the latrines. Of course there were very few water W.C.s in those days. Anyhow, I managed to steer clear of that job.

Sidney Camplejohn 1915.

Amos Camplejohn 1915.

A few days later after various roll calls and a few short route marches, I was selected along with some more of the recruits for a Motor Ambulance Unit, and we were supplied with 15 new Sunbeam ambulances that could take four stretchers or 10 sitting cases. Also there were six Ford T-type ambulances that carried two stretcher cases. Also six motor cycles, three Triumph and three Douglas. Those were the complete amount required for an Army Division, and each Division had three Field Ambulance Units. Ours turned out to be the 39th Division. The three Field Ambulance Units were 132nd, 133rd and 134th. The markings on all the vehicles in the 39th Division were similar to Sheffield Wednesday Football Club colours – blue and white stripes upright. Each ambulance had a number on the side. My number was 4, so our Field Ambulance Unit comprised of five Sunbeam, two Fords and two motor cycles. A few days after we received the ambulance we left Grove Park to Bulford Camp on Salisbury Plain. We did a bit of route marching and we slept in the ambulances. Whilst I was at Bulford I received a letter from home informing me that I was summoned to appear at a Sheffield Court in connection with the accident I had down Pitsmoor when I ran into the cows. I requested to see the Officer-in-Charge and he read the summons and gave me a warrant of leave and a railway pass for eight days, which I gladly received and went home.

A very pleasant surprise awaited me when I got home. My mother said the case had been settled and I think the farmer had agreed to pay damages to the chara, so I enjoyed my few days at home. Unfortunately the worst part of a leave is that you have to go back and Bulford Camp was not what you would call a holiday resort. It was up to the boot tops in mud and it was winter time. Every morning before breakfast a chap arrived, selling morning papers. If we were still in the ambulance he used to lift the rear flap up of the ambulance and shout out, "All about the great heat wave, one penny." That was the cost of each daily paper. We used to get one every morning. Eventually we moved from Bulford Camp and took the ambulances, motor cycles etc. to Avonmouth where they were put on a boat for Rouen in France. We all went to Southampton by train and lined up at the dockside for the boat. Whilst we were waiting we had all our equipment in our kit bag. This period was just after the song had been published, 'Pack up your Troubles in Your Old Kit Bag and Smile Boys Smile'. I don't think there were many of us that had anything to smile about. I believe it was late evening when we set sail. I had a sleep and realised the boat had been anchored just off Le Havre. It then went on to Rouen where we unloaded. We again received our ambulances ready for duty on the Western Front.

When we had everything fixed up, we proceeded through various towns and villages to Merville. There we were separated from the other two Field Ambulances, the 132nd and 134th and our 133rd Field Ambulance Unit went on to Estaires, which was a small village. The French people were still living in the houses. It was not a place that you would choose for a holiday. The only good point about it was the quiet. Later, I, along with another of our ambulances, went to a small village called La Gorgue, where we stayed a while, and one vehicle would go on duty up to the Lone Farm, Givenchy, which was an Advanced Dressing Station and it was always receiving the wounded brought in by the stretcher bearers from the trenches or aid posts. As one ambulance came down with the wounded, another one would replace it. The wounded were carried to the Casualty Clearing Station. After a while we were moved on to the Ypres section and our Advanced Dressing Station was the asylum at Ypres. Anyone approaching the Ypres sector during night time and dark would find it a terrifying experience with all the Very Lights lighting the sky both from the German trenches and ours. They called it the Horse Shoe. You were going right down the centre.

Whilst at the asylum, I with my No 4 ambulance and Charlie Connor with No. 2 ambulance, were instructed to take two loads of medical equipment to the advanced Aid Post, through Ypres, and Lille Gate to St. Jean. Passing the prison at Ypres, and approaching a section of road where a unit of our artillery used to fire into the German lines, I had often passed when they were firing and the sound used to be deafening. Unfortunately this particular night, it was the Germans that were shelling our 18-pounders and they were all exploding in the road. There were no intervals where you could get through, but owing to so much rubble in the road, I could not keep going. I had a spare driver on with me, Harry Hamer, a Lancashire lad. He got out of the ambulance front seat and shouted to me to get off as we should both get killed. Eventually I followed him a little way back and whilst we were walking back a shell burst and a piece of shrapnel went through his army great coat, but fortunately did not cause any injury. It was dark and we were sheltering as we thought. We lit a cigarette each and when we lit the match we saw that the hut was no protection whatever, as it was made of canvas.

Anyhow the shelling quietened down and we went back to the ambulance. First of all I found I had lost all the water out of the radiator and I knew we could not take the medical equipment to the Aid Post at St. Jean. Our other ambulance had gone back to our Headquarters at the asylum, and informed them that Johnny and Harry Hamer had gone West, as it appeared to him following on behind that my ambulance had got a direct hit and he was afraid they would not see us again. Before getting back into the ambulance I lifted both sides of the bonnet at the front, so that we could get as much cool air to the engine as possible. I then started the engine with the starting handle and then got into the driving seat, with my hands under the canvas shield which came over the dashboard, and fitted with an expanding spring, and came just under the driver's chin, as there were no windscreens. I put my hands in the position to grip the steering wheel. It was a four spoked wheel, but some large pieces of shrapnel must have blown the steering wheel off, and just left the centre piece of the steering wheel on the shaft. I decided to get back to the asylum which was our headquarters. I had about 250 yards to do in reverse gear which I did with gripping the centre piece and going slowly. On my way back I stopped about a quarter of an hour at the 132nd Field Ambulance. They were stationed at the prison in Ypres. That was to get the engine cooled down owing to having no water. I then had approximately one mile to the asylum. I could only go slowly, but I managed to get the ambulance into the yard at the asylum. When I arrived they had all been down in the dumps after Charlie Conner had given his report.

When we examined the ambulance next morning it had ripped some pieces out of the canvas side and top. Also it had broken some of the iron structural sections which opens out to carry stretcher cases and closes for sitting cases. The next day the vehicle was taken to the

Field Workshops and we had it back again in about three days. The engine was not damaged and everything was alright again. Evidently the Officer Commanding the Field Ambulance Unit, Colonel Bowles, instructed our Sergeant that he wanted to see me in his office to give him all the particulars. I explained to him and he complimented me on getting the ambulance back to the Headquarters. That was the last I heard concerning the escapade. Although we were often passing along the road that had been heavily shelled, we did not have any worry at that point again.

We were mostly going to the Advanced Dressing Stations at Essex Farm or Du Hallou and conveying the wounded to a Casualty Clearing Station just beyond Poperinge. During the year 1916, that was one of the most severe winters that I have ever experienced. The wounded that we were taking from different parts of the lines both on the Somme and Ypres areas, apart from their severe wounds were suffering from frostbite, and there was no heating in the ambulances. We could only put an extra blanket over them. The following year a vast improvement was made. Each ambulance was taken to the Field Workshops and fitted with exhaust pipe central heating. A special valve unit was fitted just below the exhaust manifold and a steel T-shaped pipe inside the ambulance body which was secured by steel stays or brackets and fitted to the woodwork about two inches clear of the seats, which were used when conveying sitting patients. Also was fitted a strong steel wire mesh, for safety and protection from the heated pipes. All the piping that was fitted into the ambulance body was complete with no detachable joints making it secure and safe from any exhaust gases escaping. There was a short lever attached to the unit for one position to go through the silencer and could be turned to send the exhaust gases through the inside of the ambulance and within a few minutes it would be quite warm for the wounded or sick patients that we may be conveying. Many of the wounded would often remark to the Orderly or me that they had been warmer than they had been for a long time. We realised that the heating system had been a huge success. Also when we were further away from the danger areas we used to sleep in the ambulance and if it was cold weather we had a radiator muff over the bonnet and radiator of the ambulance and if we started the engine up and ran it for two or three minutes it would be nice and warm sleeping on the stretcher. In any case we used to run the engine every night, so that it would be easy started in emergency during the night or early morning.

When we were back further from the Line, it would be more like a rest period. We would fix up for a night's pleasure. We had a small gramophone and we had some of the latest records, etc. If there were more than eight or nine of us, which would include our R.A.M.C. Orderlies, we would get two ambulances back to back with the rear flaps rolled up and a cover to stop as much draught as possible. Later in the evening we would get the Primus stoves going with bully beef, Maconochies, tins of pork and beans, cheese biscuits and various other items. The other end of the ambulances, we should have the gramophone going and some would be having a game with cards, losing or winning. Regarding the suppers that we fixed up, we do not know whether you would call it a mixed grill or not, but we used to enjoy it.

Regarding our Ambulance Drivers, they were a grand set of chaps, but most of them were lacking in experience mechanically, including the Corporals and Sergeants. They had not the slightest idea of maintenance. On the Sunbeam ambulance's dashboard, at the front of the driver was a small brass plunger which used to rise up with the oil pressure from the oil pump of the engine. The oil pump was at the bottom of the crank chamber or sub. base. There was a round filter that the oil had to pass through and during cold weather if the oil was too thick it would not get to the pump, therefore there would be no oil circulating through the crankshaft and camshaft and all the various working parts of the engine. Some of the drivers used to pull the brass plunger up with their fingers and if it did not drop down, they used to take it for granted it would be alright. This plunger is the pressure gauge for the oil as there were no other means to show that the oil was circulating through the engine.

The crank chambers or sub. were low down in the chassis and during the winter months the base, especially on the Somme, used to get about 1½ inches of mud which used to set hard almost like cement and the Sergeant was continually getting the other drivers to scrape it off and clean. I was continually telling him that mud on the crankchamber was as good as two overcoats for protection of frost etc. It would also help to keep the oil workable. I think the Sergeant realised that later, as all the other ambulances you could tell by the sounds that the engines were not running smoothly.

I remember one very difficult position that I was in. I had been instructed to go with the ambulance to pick up some stretcher cases at a particular First Aid Post approaching the Messines Ridge. To get to this point you had to drive on a sleeper track and it was very uneven and rough. I think I must have dropped across where some of the planks were missing, as I unfortunately broke the rear half of the front spring. It broke completely in two pieces. At this time I was on my own, no Orderly to help me, also I had no sick or wounded patients in the ambulance. It was a good job we always had a screw jack for lifting the ambulance. It was not what you would call a nice place as there were shells exploding around. I could not drive the ambulance without doing something. I studied the position and came to the conclusion that I could do a repair if I could get a strong piece of wood with one end slightly tapered. Fortunately I dropped across a piece, just the right length. It must have been used for a stoop to be knocked into the ground. I lifted the vehicle up with the jack underneath the chassis frame and then pushed the tapered part of the wood over the front part of the spring inside the end of the chassis and the rear part of the piece of timber fitted tight to the shackle ends at the rear. I then wrapped it round with rope over the front section of the spring.

I got the vehicle back to our Headquarters, but it was a slow job and a bumpy ride as the part where I had fitted the timber was practically under the driving seat of the ambulance. I found out later that a young man from Wombwell who was a driver in the Horse Artillery, saw me working at the ambulance but he could not stop. His name was Colin Weston, a well known Wombwell family. The next day the ambulance was taken to the Field Workshop and a new front spring was fitted. They remarked that they had not had any vehicles brought in strung up like that was.

A lot of our work was usually going to pick up wounded or sick and take them to Casualty Clearing Stations, but one particular incident was a little strange. I was instructed to take Captain Lindeman who was the Medical Officer to pick up a wounded French woman. She had been badly wounded in the abdomen and we were running round to get her into a French hospital. If I remember rightly where we got the lady to was St. Venante, but the Medical Officer told me that he did not think she would recover and we found out later that she died, as it was a very serious wound. I think she must have just previously had her supper, as the floor of the ambulance was nearly covered with peas, which she had vomited. The poor lady must have eaten a pea supper.

We had been working around the Givenchy areas and moved on to what used to be a small village called Cambrin and we parked the ambulances up on a short lane alongside the church. There were a few buildings which had been battered about a lot with German shell-fire, but some had been put to good use by previous Field Ambulance Units including one building which had been fitted up to enable the Army cooks to prepare a good midday dinner. I feel sure that our cooks had arrived a while before us that first day, as one of our other ambulance drivers was sitting in my ambulance and we decided to go to the cookhouse for our midday meal, with our plates and dixie and we got a very pleasant surprise. They had cooked some roast beef and various vegetables. It was just like a good old Yorkshire dinner. We went into my ambulance to enjoy it. Unfortunately before we could get started the R.A.M.C. Staff Sergeant came into the ambulance and told us that a wounded Royal Sussex soldier had been brought from the Line and he died on the way to the Dressing Station, and he told us to come out and give him a hand to carry him into the church which was used as a mortuary. So Griffin, our other driver, and myself left our dinner on the seats in the ambulance. Griffin got his hands under the shoulders and the Staff Sergeant got hold of his feet and I put my hands underneath middle of his back and we carried him into the church and placed him on a duck board, ready for burial in the churchyard when the Padre was available. The dead boy I don't think would be more than 18 or 19 years of age. He had a rosy complexion and ginger hair. After we had completed that unfortunate job I looked at my hands and they were covered with blood, which was still warm. I don't think he could have died until they got him almost to the church. Anyhow the first job I then had to do was give my hands a good wash and then went along with Griffin to get my Yorkshire Dinner which was stone cold, but we ate it alright.

Whenever we moved to a new place, we usually went scouting round for anything special. Well, there was something very unusual about the Church as it had been struck by an unexploded shell from the German lines which had penetrated the high part of the rear wall and made a large gaping hole and the nose part of the shell went through the front of the church and stuck with the nose of the shell showing outside of the church with the base of the shell showing inside the church very near to the entrance. The part of the church where we placed the dead soldier was only a few feet from that shell. Where the shell passed through the rear end, there was still the crucifix standing, but I could not see that standing. This crucifix must have been reset as it was only fastened on to the broken part of the wall on one corner.

We did not stay long at Cambrin. We were moved to Essars and our field ambulances were at a small village called La Gorge, and continually going up to Lone Farm and Givenchy, which was the Advanced Dressing Station. One of our ambulances used to stay overnight at that place and we were usually kept busy taking the wounded to the Casualty Clearing Station just beyond Popperinge. One particular day I had been on duty taking wounded from Lone Farm and taking wounded down the lane. I met going towards Lone Farm an Officer in charge of a firing party. There were two soldier prisoners walking up the lane in between the firing party and following behind was Charlie Connor driving behind slowly. He was also going on night duty at the Advanced Dressing Station. The two prisoners were fixed up at a special place made up by the engineers and all the personnel at the Dressing Station had been instructed and warned that they must not go near the prisoners or communicate with them in any way. Next morning in the early hours the prisoners were taken out and shot. The Staff at the Ambulance Station could hear the Command Officer giving the orders, which would have been a memory which they will never forget.

Later on we were on the move again and finished up at Bethune. We had been there previously and we always considered Bethune a nice place to stay like home from home, where we were billeted at the college, which was quite near to the 33rd Casualty Clearing Station. On the Sunday in August, I believe it was August 1917, a large number of the very high ranking officers from the Western Front met at the Square in Bethune for a conference. We did not see much of that, as those things were kept secret. As far as we knew there was nothing went off that day to disturb them as everything was very quiet.

But the following day, 7th August, being Bank Holiday Monday, the Germans started shelling Bethune, and they must have been using a rather heavy type of shell. One shell got a direct hit on the 33rd Advanced Dressing Station, and injured a number of the Nursing Staff and wounded patients. We evacuated some of them to another Clearing Station. Also the Square, which was usually occupied on Monday mornings by the various French Traders as Market Day, there were many shells exploded in that place which was called Belfry Square. I was instructed to take my ambulance with an R.A.M.C. Sergeant and four

R.A.M.C. stretcher bearers and go into the Square to collect the wounded. I drove just inside the Square and the five R.A.M.C. went into the Square to seek out any casualties. My Orderly who at that time was called Alf Frazer, we sat down in the ambulance, but immediately a Military Police man came to me and remarked where we were standing in the Square was dangerous and said, "Draw your ambulance a bit further away down the road," which we did. A few minutes later my four stretcher bearers came to get the four stretchers from the ambulance. Alf handed two and I the other two. The last person that I handed the stretcher to was struck by shrapnel from a shell that burst practically in the same spot where I had parked the ambulance. I always considered that Military Policeman saved my life and my Orderly's. I hope the Policeman did not stay in the same place. The R.A.M.C. stretcher bearer who died from wounds was Private P. A. Brown.

Later that day we cleared away the bodies in the ambulances. If I remember rightly I think I carried about ten or twelve, mostly French civilians, on the stretchers. I remember one journey whilst on this work, my Orderly opened the connection window and requested me to stop and come round to the rear of the ambulance to show me one of the bodies which had a very open wound and part of his inside was hanging over the side of the stretcher. Between us we pushed everything back and turned the body partly sideways and carried on to the destination which was a French burial place. Later on we got back to our Headquarters, the college in Bethune. I think I can say that particular day was the worst day that we ever had at Bethune, and the remaining period became quiet, but we were not long before we were moving to another section which was again on the Somme. Fortunately the removal to that area must have been changed from Headquarters and we finally arrived in the Popperinge district and I was one of the fortunate to get leave home. I don't recollect the period but I believe it was either nine or ten days, which was approximately 21 months after the leave I got whilst in England. There were a few of the R.A.M.C. also got leave from our Field Ambulance Section and one Mechanical Transport Dispatch Rider named Alec Jackson from the 132nd Field Ambulance. His home was at Keighley, Yorkshire and we went together to Calais and London. Alec Jackson was previously a Tester for the Scott Motor Cycle Company at Bradford. I should describe Alec as the finest motor cycle rider I have ever seen.

However we arrived at Calais and got on the boat and I think it was one of the roughest trips I have ever had on the sea. It must have been a very old boat, and we were sitting sideways and the back rest was a kind of board, and to keep on our seats we had to put our arms behind the board to hold on. There was a full boat load of soldiers going on leave and the sea was that rough practically everyone was sick and with the boat tilting so much we were getting a tremendous pressure on the back rest board. Finally it came adrift and we all slid right across the bottom of the boat to the other side.

We eventually arrived at Dover, but it was a while before the boat could pull into the dock to unload, but we managed it at last, and got off and there was the passenger train. We had not many yards to walk, but the wind and rain were terrific. When I got into the railway carriage, I looked into the mirror and my face was red on one side and white on the other. That was with walking the short distance from boat to train in the rain and severe wind. We had not many minutes to wait before the train was on its way to Waterloo Station and when we arrived there I was feeling rather hungry for something to eat, so I went first of all into the restaurant and had a feed.

Before I left France my friend Charlie Connor asked me to call and see his wife Maud, as I had been with Charlie on two or three evening visits when we were stationed at Grove Park, before we went over to France, so I got a taxi at the station and told the driver to drop me off at the address in Camberwell. I probably stayed about half an hour. I had to have a cup of tea and told Charlie's wife that he was O.K. and not to worry.

I then got a taxi to take me to St. Pancras station. When I arrived there, I was still feeling hungry so I had another meal there before getting on the train to Sheffield. I then got a train to Wombwell Main station and eventually walked home to Darfield. It was a very pleasant surprise for my mother and father and all the family. I had a good night's rest and a good breakfast the following morning. The first day I had a good run round to see various friends and relatives, and I was very surprised when I saw the queues at the food shops and various grocery stores, and realised how difficult it must have been. I told my mother that she must not send any more parcels to me in France as we could probably have been more able at times to send them something.

I remember one evening whilst at home, my father and brother were explaining to me about an experience they had had recently when a German Zeppelin came over and most people, including my father and brother, left their homes and ran away up the fields for safety. I remarked, "What did you run there for?" and one of them said, "You would have gone if they had been as near to you." I told them if the Germans dropped anything at Darfield, they would only be dropping it to find out if it was a good one or not.

One morning whilst on leave, I decided to have a run out to Woodlands and Doncaster to see a few friends. On the route that we used to operate there were now trams running between Woodlands and Doncaster. I decided to go to the point where we used to start at the Doncaster end, that was the Bay Horse Hotel on the Great North Road, and the trams used the same. Whilst watching one of the trams standing for passengers, I noticed a lady get in and sit down in the tram where they sat sideways. Suddenly I noticed this particular person's mouth sending a tremendous amount of blood as though it was being pumped out. She must have been dead within two minutes. They came with a stretcher and took her to the Guild Hall, which is only about one hundred yards further into Doncaster. I did not stay long at Doncaster, and decided to come back home.

One evening whilst on leave I decided to go and see our local Doctor, Daniel Foley, as he knew the history of the kidney trouble that I very often suffered, and I told him that every time I reported sick in France they gave me medicine and duty, sometimes gave me a couple of No. 9s and that was it. Dr. Dan said he would give me a Doctor's Certificate and the symptoms he described were that I was suffering from Renal Callouses. He said ,"Whenever you are ill; show this to your Medical Officer."

Well, the days seemed to be passing away quickly. I think I spent most of the time visiting. I had one weekend at home. On a Saturday the passenger vehicles operated the service from Darfield to Wombwell and Barnsley, and one of my younger brothers, Arthur, but who we always called Bob, was driving one of the charas this particular Saturday. According to form, he had not a very good record, as I was informed he broke down practically every Saturday. Of course he had not had a lot of experience as he worked at Houghton Main Colliery and only drove a bit at weekends. So this Saturday I decided that I would relieve him and drive in his place, which I did and carried on right to the finish without any trouble. They chalked it up at the front end of the garage, 'Bob has worked all through without a breakdown'. That chalk marking was still on the wall for a very long period.

I consider that the days that I was on leave were mostly spent on visiting friends and relatives as there were a lot of them. Eventually it was getting near to the end of my home leave and my mother was very much concerned and worried about me going back. I made a quick good-bye all round and set off to Wombwell Main station. I did not get any more leave. It's nice getting home but not so leaving. I had a decent journey going back to Sheffield and St. Pancras and one to Dover and Calais where I had to report to the R.T.O., (Railway Transport Officer), for travel arrangements to our Division which was the 39th. I was instructed to get on a passenger train. I believe it was to Abbeville. We then got on an Army lorry which took us to Popperinge where I again joined up with our Field Ambulances. We did eventually get down on to the Somme again. We actually finished up at the same section of the Line with our ambulances parked up at a point approaching Aveloy Wood and we usually had two or three of us with the ambulances at the Advanced Dressing Station which was through Aveloy Wood at Beaumont Hamel.

We used to be kept busy with taking the wounded to the Casualty Clearing Stations after they had been having their wounds treated by the Medical Officer. At this Advanced Dressing Station we slept in dugouts. I don't think I have mentioned it before, but putting it bluntly, we were all lousy, including Officers. Also in these dugouts they were infested with rats. I have known times many when we have been laid on these temporary beds with a blanket over us. I have felt the rats running over the top of the blanket. They seemed to be about tame.

Late one night whilst at this dugout one of our ambulances had to take two stretcher cases to the Casualty Clearing Station and Charlie Connor who was along with me and it was his turn to do this journey. Unfortunately it was a very foggy night and Charlie set off with this load and he had only gone a few yards and he came back to me in the dugout and he was very upset as he had bumped into our drinking water cart. I saw the state he was in and said, "Get down here Charlie, I will take them." Of course Charlie was an experienced London taxi driver, but he had not the same experience that I had with all sorts of conditions on country roads and lanes.

Another particular journey that Charlie had to take to the Casualty Clearing Station, I believe there was a bit of fog. He remarked to the Sergeant that he had come through a lot of shell fire and he thought some parts of the shrapnel had struck the ambulance, so the Sergeant thought he would have a look round the next morning, which he did. The Sergeant was a Yorkshire man. His home was Bradford. After looking round the ambulance he then saw Charlie and remarked to him, "By gum Charlie, Germans must be hard up as they have started sending wooden shells over." Charlie had evidently been getting off the road and running into some tree stumps as the Sergeant had found some wooden splinters on the structural parts of the ambulance.

Whilst on this Section I came off duty from the Advanced Dressing Station Dugouts on to the part where we parked the ambulances. I was taking some sick patients and saw a Dennis lorry coming towards me, and I noticed the driver had a red thin scarf or handkerchief round his neck. I thought the only person that I remember like that was Albert Greenhow who was the first person to drive the first bus for Greenhows at Darfield when they used to take miners from Wombwell and Darfield to Houghton Main Pit. Surprisingly, it was Albert, but he had not noticed me. A day or two later I was busy repairing a couple of inner tubes as we got a fair amount of punctures whilst on the Somme. I again saw two or three Dennis lorries heading towards me. I eventually spotted Albert on one of these lorries which were going to a Ration Dump which was at the approach to Aveloy Wood. It would be approximately 300 yards down the road, so I decided to leave the inner tube repairing job and go and see Albert. I sat on the front seat of his lorry and we had a good chat about old times at home. Whilst I was talking to him a mule transport wagon bumped into his front offside mudguard. I left Albert playing hell up with him. That was the last time I saw Albert Greenhow. It was not many days after, that I had a letter from home telling me that Albert had got killed.

We stayed awhile in that area and I saw where a Dennis lorry had been struck by shellfire and badly shattered, and I thought that could possibly have been the lorry that Albert had been driving. We stayed awhile longer and we were continually taking the wounded from the Beaumont Hamel Advanced Dressing Station. Whenever the troops or battalions were changing over, which they did periodically, they very often used to make a short rest in Aveloy Wood. This was usually in the middle of the night and they used to lie down on the ground at the sides of the road. As we were running without lights we could not see them and the only way we could spot them, was to see a small light lighting the cigarettes, as practically all of them used to manage to get a smoke when they were resting.

Later our Division was moved away from the Somme, to the Peronne area. During our period in the Peronne district I suffered a very severe attack of my kidney trouble and I had been vomiting very much and after this particular bout I was passing blood with my urine. So I decided to get a sample in a bottle and took it to our Medical Officer and it was like pure blood. He immediately fixed up with one of our own ambulances and sent me to the Base Hospital at Rouen where I was admitted. During this period the Germans were advancing in certain parts on the Western Front and the Base Hospital had most of its male nursing staff removed to go into the fighting units. I myself whenever I had finished the following days, I would feel quite normal again. I was examined various times and had one or two X-rays which did not show anything wrong with the kidney.

I did not stay in bed and I kept helping in the ward which had approximately 45 beds. It got to the position that all the wounded and sick patients were calling me orderly and I came to the conclusion I was doing more work in the hospital than I usually did. I was called on by all the patients even during the night. They would shout out, “Orderly, bring me a water bottle or a bedpan.” I used to help with the meals, some would be on a diet, some no diet at all.

I also used to help the Sister by the name of Henderson. She was unmarried, a very kind Scottish lady. Her father was a General in the Army. She used to go round with the Medical Officer who was a Surgeon and he used to perform some of the operations in the ward. I remember one operation that the Surgeon was performing on a wounded soldier who had a rather nasty gash on his right hand side groin, and the Sister was giving him the anaesthetic, and she requested me to hold his right leg steady whilst the Surgeon was doing the cutting or trimming of the wound. I had never seen an operation before and whilst the Surgeon was doing his work, the soldier started singing, “Yip I Yaddy I Hey, I Hey.” It sounded to me funny, but it was serious and the Sister remarked, “Why do the Germans injure them in such awful places?” I should imagine he would be sent over to England. I feel sure he would eventually get something like normal again.

I believe I only stayed at the Base Hospital about two weeks, then was put into the Mechanic Transport Depot in Rouen. There was a lot of red tape there, parading and guard duties, and I was pleased when I was detailed to take a Vauxhall touring car to the Seventh Corps Headquarters to a place called Houle. At this particular place they had a number of Staff cars; including one for the Corps Commander whose name was General Snow. I was put in what they call the Pool. I was acting as a spare. Whenever one of the cars had to go into the workshop for the usual service, I should be called to take their place. This Vauxhall that I was driving was a 4-seater tourer and carried two spare wheels. It was a very nice car to drive and very reliable.

I believe I took the General out on two occasions and each time they would take the radiator cap off and put another radiator cap fitted with the General’s Corps Commander’s flag, which was a red one with a white cross in the centre. Also they would clip on a klaxon horn which you could turn with a handle. You had only to give it a turn and any vehicles ahead of you whether horse drawn or motor vehicles would get well on the right hand side when they heard that noise, or turned round and saw the flag showing at the front. You did not get any obstructions whatever. It was nice, easy driving. I always found from my experience that the higher ranking officers always treated you more as an equal and the lower graded, like Second Lieutenants up to Captains tried to treat you as dirt.

Whilst at the Seventh Corps Headquarters at Houle, I very often used to get the job of taking the Officers to Calais or Boulogne, when they were going on leave to England and it was usually a stay for a few hours at one of these places. I should be instructed to bring back any Officers that were returning from their home leave, and I usually got a reasonably good tip from the Officers I was taking on leave. This was a job that I really did enjoy doing. Except one particular journey. I was taking a very high ranking Officer on leave and on my journey to Calais, I was stopped by a Military Policeman who was checking the speeds of vehicles. I had to give him particulars of name, Unit and place where stationed, and he told me I should be reported to the Camp Commandant of the Seventh Corps Headquarters for doing a speed of 58 miles per hour. A few days later, I was charged and had to go under escort to the Camp Commandant. To my surprise the Officer had received a letter from the Officer that I had taken to Calais, stating that he had requested me to push on as he wanted to be sure of getting on the boat in time. Therefore my case was dismissed. That was proof which I mentioned earlier, this Officer sent that letter explaining my case which I appreciated. Had it been a Lieutenant or Captain, they would not have bothered.

Whilst being at this Headquarters during any leisure time there was an Estamina where they had a billiard table. I believe it was practically full size, but the most peculiar thing about it was that it had no pockets and I, along with some of the other Staff Drivers, used to spend a fair amount of time at this table and we used to play Cush-Cannons and that used to make it a very skilful game. I had a reasonable amount of playing at Billiards previously in England and could hold my own when playing with most of the Staff. Anyhow it used to make some of the evenings very enjoyable. It made you think that there was not a war on sometimes.

I had another special troublesome journey when I was taking one of the top Officers and a Captain along with him, they did not tell me where they were going. It was early one afternoon. They got into the car and I had not gone much more than a mile and I had a puncture. This Vauxhall 25 h.p. car had two spare wheels. Both the two Officers got out of the car and the Chief said to his understudy, "Come on, we will be walking on and the driver can pick us up after he gets the wheel changed." On this Vauxhall car which had wire spoked wheels it did not take much more than a minute to get it jacked up and the only part that you had to remove to get the wheel off was a locking ring which was shaped with two strong lugs. All you had to do was to give the lug a sharp tap with the hammer, and then you could turn the locking ring off with your fingers and the wheel would slide off quite easily. At the nut ends were what is called a splined fitting, and the splines on the wheels would be inwardly. Putting the wheel back on, you had only to just push it on and it would go easily. To position them you would screw the ring on as far as you could with your fingers, then give it a pretty hard sharp tap on to one of the lugs, then it would be quite safe to proceed on your journey. This was not the only puncture I had on the journey. I had two more and after the second puncture I had no more wheels left. Fortunately the next must have been a slow puncture as I managed to get a fair amount of air into it with the hand pump. Anyhow, I managed to scramble back to the Headquarters with no complaints from the Officers.

One of the high ranking Officers at Headquarters, I believe he was a Lieutenant-General – all the Staff Drivers used to call him General Knapp. He had a car and driver whom all the other drivers used to feel sorry for, as this General was fearless himself. If they were shelling an area, this Officer would instruct the driver to go right up to the danger zone, and then get out and tell the driver to stay there. The other drivers used to say he was a very clever man especially on unexploded shells. They used to say he always had a good idea on the distances etc. I took him out twice whilst I was on that Staff and all the conversation I got was, "Drive on," and, "Stop here." He left the car a few times, but I had to stop in the car, whenever he got out. You could not call him a cheerful officer. I was pleased when his car and driver started again, and I never had the pleasure of taking him out after that.

Whilst I was out with another Staff Officer I had stopped at a place where the Officer went to another Unit, and whilst I was waiting in the car, one of our ambulances stopped as the driver had spotted me, and we had a chat for about five minutes. Evidently this driver must have told the Sergeant of the 133rd Field Ambulance where I had been previously that he had seen me, and I was driving a Vauxhall car and attached to Seven Corps Headquarters at Houle. The Sergeant informed Colonel Miller who was the Commander of the Field Ambulance that he would be pleased if he could get me back again to my old Field Ambulance Unit. Colonel Miller sent a dispatch to the Corps Commander with this request. Of course I did not know anything about it until I was instructed to go to the Camp Commandant's Office and he told me about this request, and he gave me the option. I was quite welcome to stay at Seven Corps Headquarters, or I could go back to my old Unit. I told him I would be pleased to join up again. The transfer was granted and I then went back again driving the same ambulance that I had been driving previously.

Whilst I had been away, there had been a few Honours granted. Our Sergeant, I could not call him brave, but he was presented with the D.C.M., and two of the drivers. Matthew Cousins, he drove a Ford T-Type ambulance and he always drove the Head of our Field Ambulance Units who was Assistant Director of Medical Services. Matthew was presented with the Military Medal. My old pal Charlie Connor received the Military Medal also. It was not long after getting back that our 39th Division had been in so many battles and lost so many men that it was to be disbanded and the remaining soldiers transferred to other Divisions. Our field ambulances were attached to an American Division, but the main Officers including the Colonel-in-Command of the Ambulances stayed with us. We had a few American Medical Officers added on to our Unit, but when we went further up the Line to collect wounded and sick, there were then mostly Yanks.

Later on, we started moving the Germans back and we were beginning to get into sections of ground that the Germans had been holding and we seemed to be moving fast, as we no sooner got to a place before we were moving on again. I remember one morning, we had just moved forward a few miles and it was a section that we had never been to before and stopped at a place which must have been a small village at some time. We had only just stopped and the Sergeant came to me and told me that Major Warwick, who was the Officer-in-Charge of our Field Ambulances, wanted me to take an Officer of the Engineers to where he required to go, as Major Warwick wanted the place where the Officer of the Engineers had been staying. Within a few minutes the Officer came out with his luggage etc. comprising of two very large valises along with his Batman and his kit. Then we set off. I did not know the name of the place where we had started from. I followed the Officer's instructions and kept going. I knew it had very recently been ground held by the Germans.

Whilst going along these narrow lanes, this particular section of the road, the left hand side was banked up, sloping to about three or four feet high and all along this banking the Germans must have dug. I should imagine there must have been two or three hundred bodies. I did not see any British bodies, mostly German and French. The trenches that they had dug were prepared to roll each body into the trench, then cover them up with earth, but evidently, they must have had to move away very quickly, before they could complete these burials. I do not know the distance of these trenches and bodies, but it must have been at least half a mile.

Well, we kept on going and I was wondering how I should find my way back, as we had left the road in a lot of districts and seemed to be going across country. Eventually, we arrived at a place where there was a Chateau in some grounds. The Officer and the Batman got out of the ambulance, but they left their luggage and equipment inside the ambulance. A little while later the Batman came back to the ambulance to let me know that they were examining the Chateau seeking bombs as they were expecting it going up at any time and requested me to keep the luggage in the ambulance. When he had gone away I studied things out and I came to the conclusion that if that building was likely to go up I should probably go up with it. I knew that we were winning the war and we were not supposed to transport anyone except wounded or sick or connected with the medical services. Therefore I got all of the equipment out of the ambulance and put it on the ground and I went away with the ambulance. I felt sure that they would be staying at this Chateau, and my job was to find my way back to I did not know where. I felt like a pigeon flying round to get my bearings. I did not follow the same way back as I moved more on to the right and thought I was going in the right direction. I got on a kind of lane and whilst proceeding on here the lane at one point dropped down to a low part and there was a kind of ravine where the road seemed to drop down and it must have filled with water during wet weather and at the bottom of this ravine there were approximately eight or nine German bodies and they looked as if they had been there a few days. Any vehicles going along this lane were forced to run over them, which I was also obliged to do.

After going through this Section I was driving along, when suddenly a Medical Officer came out of a little dugout and requested me to stop as he had a wounded soldier in his dugout, which was an aid post. He told me to take this wounded soldier to our 133rd Field Ambulance. This Officer knew where our place was. I explained to him I had had to come away in the morning that day and I did not know the place. He directed me and on my way, I got on to a main road and it was like coming from a race meeting. There was a convoy of lorries loaded with women and children. They were all shouting and cheering. I was told later that they were from a part of Alsace Lorraine which had been released from that part of the country which the Germans had overrun in a previous war.

I did eventually get to our Advanced Dressing Station where they received the wounded soldier. I than had tea along with our other ambulance drivers as it was late afternoon. After tea three of us decided to have a scout round the village. I don't think anyone knew the name of the place. However, we got into one building which had been a house at some time and some of the Germans had been staying inside. Also, there must have been French civilians previously, as we found some old clothing. The most comical item that I was interested in was a German comic magazine. It was one of the funniest I have ever seen. The Germans must have had some very amusing periods, reading and seeing the various pictures which were performed to the detriment of the British. Whilst I was looking through the magazine I saw a complete page on Lloyd George who was the British Prime Minister during the 1914-18 war, and it was showing where they had a greasy pole and it had been forced through Lloyd George's mouth and out through his back passage, and he was being carried by two German soldiers, one at each end of the pole. The Germans were goose stepping him and they appeared by their expression that they were proud to be doing this job. I must say it was an exact description with the typical civilian clothing he normally wore. It was clever, but very vulgar. I pulled the complete page out of this book and kept if for a considerable time and later decided to tear it up.

When we came away from the old building, we joined all our other pals. One of the lads that went along with me looking through this old building was George Linfoot. His home was Dewsbury, Yorkshire and he was always to the front in playing his part to get a good laugh. He had brought out of this house a black fur, and an old jacket and trousers. All our drivers were billeted in a fairly large room and in one end of this room was a bed with an iron framed bedstead. Our Sergeant, Peel, who was a Bradford man, claimed that bed for himself. The Sergeant had gone out, I expect to join some of the other Sergeants and other ranks. Whilst he was away, we decided to dress George Linfoot up as an old Frenchman. We got some medical adhesive tape and fitted George up with a black moustache and pointed beard, and when we had finished him he looked a typical Froggy.

When the Sergeant came in it would be almost midnight and he had been where they had plenty to drink, in other words he was drunk. We had got George in his bed and we told the Sergeant that this old Frenchman had been playing hell up stating that the bed that the Sergeant was claiming was his bed. The Sergeant leaned over and told the Frenchman in Yorkshire – English – French, "Vous stay issy messeur." The next morning when the Sergeant discovered who the old Frenchman was, he nearly went mad.

Earlier that same evening two or three American soldiers wanted to know where they could get some drinking water, and we advised them to ask the old Frenchman, which of course was George. As I mentioned earlier, we were at this time attached to an American Division with our Ambulance Unit and we were having more contacts with the American soldiers, and of course most of the Yanks classed the British as an inferior nation to theirs. Anyhow, two of the Yanks started asking the old Frenchman where they could obtain water and it was rather laughable to see and hear them trying to describe in Yankie French. After a while the old Frenchman said in broad Yorkshire, "Oh, tha' wants some watter?" Of course we had a water cart very near. I don't think there was anything else that day as it had been a long one.

Later we moved to various places and the American Division we were attached to seemed to be in a backward area. We were not now as far forward as most of the main British Division. There were a lot of rumours and a feeling that the war was coming to an end, and the Germans were on the point of surrendering, which they soon did. I believe it was 11.00am on the 11th November 1918 that the Armistice was signed. That was the end of hostilities. That morning everyone was in a very merry mood, and most of the ambulance drivers and orderlies were celebrating. They had managed to get some drink. Unfortunately late in the afternoon, I had one of the bouts of kidney trouble, so I went into the ambulance and got on a stretcher. I was in agony, but I could hear all the merriment and activity outside with my colleagues.

I remember quite well one of the drivers, Eric Craft, a Hull lad, he was not used to getting much drink but he had on this occasion. He remarked to Harry Hamer, "I want to be sick and can't." Harry Hamer, a Lancashire lad said, "Put thi finger down thi throit." Eric replied, "Which finger?" Harry replied, "Longest bugger tha's got." Although I was feeling terrible, I managed to raise a smile. I was alright again the following morning.

We moved a little and the work with the ambulances was mostly conveying sick. It would be probably five or six weeks after the Armistice was signed that we all went with our ambulances to a place called Wissant which is on the coast near Calais, where we handed in all the ambulances. We all got split up and I was again given a Vauxhall touring car and instructed to take it to the rail head at Abbeville. When I got there the car was loaded on to a flat railway truck. I had all my kit with me and was informed that I was going to Marseilles. I had a small primus stove for if I needed to make some tea. This touring car had a canvas hood which I pulled over for protection from rain and made myself as comfortable as possible for the night. During the night I could feel them doing a lot of shunting but I did not bother. I kept in the back seat and thought to myself, "I shall get somewhere." I felt the train moving along and about 6.00am the following morning, it had stopped and I noticed that there was a terrible noise as though there were a large number of people's voices, but there was nothing that I could understand. When I got out of my sleeping quarters, (the car), the train driver had stopped and all along the line, there were Indian soldiers having a conversation and I expect it was a stop for convenience, as all these troops were travelling on that train not first class, but in cattle trucks.

I got off my truck and looked at the train of mostly cattle trucks with one passenger carriage which was only occupied by a military officer, a Captain and his Batman (British). He was in charge of all the Indians on this train. Of course there would be Indian Sergeants and Corporals. Anyhow, this Officer noticed me and he would know I was on the truck with the car, and he very kindly invited me to join him in the passenger coach. So I found him very friendly and we got on very well together, which made the remaining part of the journey to Marseilles very enjoyable.

We arrived at Marseilles alright, and at the railhead they lifted the car off the truck and I was instructed to take the car to a large hotel at Aix les Bains, which was approximately twelve kilometres journey from Marseilles. This hotel was occupied by the British Military, and the person that I had to report to was the Chief Officer of the Purchase Supplies Department, and that was the Officer I was to take out daily. I used to take him all over Southern France. I lived in the same room as his Batman and we got very friendly. I did not know first of all what that Officer's job was, as some journeys were fairly long, and he would be away from the car sometimes two hours, but I learned from his Batman he was going to various districts purchasing sheep to feed the Indian troops as there were a tremendous amount of Indians camped around Marseilles. I enjoyed this work, but it did not last many weeks.

One particular day, we had been a fairly long journey and on the return, the Officer directed me into some grounds and we stopped. The Officer got out of the car and went inside the building which appeared to be a large hotel and restaurant. I stayed in the car awhile and came to the conclusion that he had gone into this place for lunch, but shortly after the Commissionaire at the hotel came to me in the car and told me to go with him. He took me into a very large dining room, where all the tables were set out for diners, but at the time

I sat down there was no one else there, so I received some very good service. I had a full lunch. There must have been approximately five or six courses and one particular course seemed to interest me more than anything else, that was frog pie. I ate it and I must say, I had never had anything like that before, but after you have eaten all sorts of meals during three to four years in the Army, you get used to eating anything. I must say it was very tasty. I ate it all except one of the frog's feet, which I was saving as a souvenir for awhile but threw it away later. I can state that I had a very good lunch and enjoyed it.

I then took the Officer back to Headquarters at Aix les Bains. I think the Officer must have completed his duties, as I was instructed to take the car and report to the Transport Depot at Marseilles, where they took in the car and I was put on duty driving a Dennis Army lorry. The work that we were usually on was going to the docks at Marseilles and loading up with all the luggage and equipment of the soldiers coming over from the Dardanelles or Mesopotamia. We usually carried about six men on the top of the luggage to help with unloading when we got them to a rest camp which was approximately three miles outside of Marseilles, where they would probably stay for a few days and then be sent back to England. A large number of them would be for demob or discharge. We were doing this kind of work almost daily. I remember one morning going to the dockside waiting for a boat to dock, and had to wait a bit longer than usual owing to the boat being late, and I noticed a French horse cab and driver who had been waiting all the time that I had been there. Eventually the boat arrived and a British Officer was one of the first to get away from the boat. He got into the cab with his fairly large valise and the French cabby got on to the front of the cab, got hold of the reins of the horse ready to drive away and the horse dropped down dead. I had been looking at this horse awhile and I came to the conclusion that it looked as if it had seen more dinner times than dinners. I always considered while I had been in France that most of the French people were rather cruel with dumb animals.

On one of these later journeys to the docks for a load of equipment and luggage and the usual about seven or eight soldiers on the top of the lorry, I was proceeding along one of the main and busiest streets. There were trams running through this street which was called Rue de la Cannibre. Whilst going along this road I had to make a quick stop owing to other vehicles on that part of the road. I was on a slight decline and in stopping the lorry, the reverse gear went into mesh, which then put the vehicle into two gears and made it impossible to move. I was holding the trams up as I was on the tram lines. The tram driver came and was playing hell up. He wanted to push the lorry forward with his tram. I could not understand what he was saying but I recognised one word which sounded like 'obstinate'. I tried to let him know that he had not to try and push the lorry at all. I got all my men from the top of the lorry, took the hand brake off and explained to them that I wanted them to push the lorry to move it just two or three inches, and that would take the weight off the gears in the gear box. I took the floor board out of the front of the lorry and just pushed the selector arm for the reverse gear back with my fingers, then got into the cab again. I put the handbrake on, started the engine, and told the soldiers to get back on top of the lorry. Then off we went with no more trouble.

Whilst I was on this work, there was a lorry driver called Billie Woodhouse whose home was somewhere just outside Leeds, and I got friendly with him and we very often used to have a walk into Marseilles and finish up at a small café very near to our Transport Depot. We would manage to get a reasonably good supper of steak and chips. Just below this café at the far end of a long yard was an abattoir and one morning when both our vehicles were not on duty, we decided to go and have a look round the abattoir. We went past the café and right to the bottom of the yard. On the way down we saw, I believe there were six live horses. Approximately five or six yards further on was one horse dead, and it appeared to us that it was a shame if they had killed this horse, as you could not see any bones sticking out and it looked perfect. Anyhow we went right into the main part of the abattoir where there were women washing and cleaning the remains of the horses. We did not stay long inside. When we came out the same way we had gone in we noticed the horse that was down had been taken away and the six horses that had been standing were down and out. We saw the reason why the dead horse had looked fat and in good condition. When he killed them, the slaughterer would cut a slit into the hide and then push the nozzle of a foot pump under the skin and start pumping, which would fill the animal to its full normal size. This would enable them to remove the hide more easily. After we had seen the carry on in the abattoirs and the yard, we never frequented the café again.

Billy Woodhouse and I were having a walk round in Marseilles one evening and he remarked to me that the clutch on his lorry was slipping badly. It was a Halley vehicle of Scottish manufacture, and I advised him that we would go into a French Chemist shop and try to get some powdered rosin or starch either of which was suitable and would do away with the slipping clutch. That type of clutch was leather to metal. The oil from the engine etc. gets on to the leather lining and any of those items would dry the leather lining. However Billie went into the shop and I stood in the doorway. It was rather amusing to see him demonstrating to the Chemist and he had not the slightest idea what he was talking about. Eventually he got a cardboard box down from a shelf, but the goods inside the box were nothing connected with what we required, so we came back empty handed. I believe we finished up with putting some powdered dust on his clutch.

We stayed together a little while and I was doing the journeys to the docks bringing back luggage and equipment up to the rest camp. Whilst at Marseilles I had a very severe attack of kidney trouble and was sent on a hospital boat to England and finished up at a very large hospital at Epsom. Before getting off the boat I had to get back on the stretcher, although I had been walking around whilst on the voyage. On arrival at the hospital in Epsom, I was put into bed. Of course I was feeling quite well in every way as I always did after an attack.

Whilst at this hospital some of the very highly qualified surgeons and physicians examined me and I also had X-rays there which as usual came out negative. They fixed me up with what they called Hospital Blues, which you could wear outside the grounds of the hospital, and during my stay there I was helping in the ward washing up and all sorts of jobs. There were a tremendous amount of patients going about on wheel chairs; some of them with both legs taken off, but they all seemed cheerful.

I got very friendly with one young man who had both his legs missing and the work that he was doing before the war was working in the horse racing stables for Lord Glanely whose place I believe was not far from Epsom. When I was admitted into that hospital, I believe it was some time in May 1919 and it was just approaching what they called the Derby Week. I talked a number of times to this young man and he told me that Lord Glanely had two horses running in the Derby and the information that he told me was if the weather was dry the stable staff thought the horse called Buchan stood a good chance, but if it was wet and the ground soft, the horse called Grand Parade would win or be very near. I wrote a letter home to my brother Amos as he was interested in horse racing and told him to back Grand Parade, also to put ten shillings on for mother. Amos backed it, but mother would not let him put anything on for her. The horse won the Derby. I just can't remember the price, whether it was 28-to-1 or 33-to-1. My brother Amos had a good win and it would be a needy case, as he had just got demobbed after being in Salonika all through his war service.

During the Race Week we had permission to go in the Hospital Blues to the race course, which would probably be about half an hour's walk, and there was a small portion allocated for the hospital patients (free), very near to what they call on the course Tattenham Corner, which is about another half mile to walk. Well I went to the course on the Tuesday and I am afraid I did not have a good day. I lost a few bob. I went again on the Wednesday and thought, "I shall win a bit on Grand Parade." As I was walking up the course the Bookies' boards were quoting Grand Parade at odds varying between 26-to-1 to 30-to-1. I thought I would wait until I got to the part of the course which we had to go to, as there would be more bookmakers up there, and I got a shock. I could not find any bookmaker with the price above 12 or 14 to 1. I finished up not backing it at all. So the Derby to me was not as beneficial as it should have been.

A few days after the Race Week I was sent to somewhere in the London area, and eventually demobilised. I got my Discharge Papers and a warrant for railway travel home. I got there alright and what a relief to be able to go where you wanted. My mother and father were very pleased. A few weeks before I came out of the Army, my father had written me a letter informing me that one of my uncles, T. S. Camplejohn, wanted to sell his share of the business of Camplejohn Brothers for the sum of £1,000. As all our family had been working and assisting in many ways we never had any financial interest in the business. When I wrote back I told my father to go ahead and I would put what money I could find to help the situation. So we agreed to purchase that third share. My father had not much money available as he had used his money up with the Picture Palace venture. I do not know if I mentioned earlier about the payments my brother Amos and myself made. The mechanical transport drivers pay was six shillings per day, and we both allocated four shillings a day to mother at home, and we kept two shillings a day for ourselves. I know for a fact that my mother was having a very difficult time all through the war in making ends meet, as she had a large family at home. Both Amos and myself got a shock when my mother told us both that the money that we had allocated for her use, she had put it all away and she insisted that we had it, which was £250 each. We reluctantly took it, which played a big part in the purchase towards the £1,000 we required. Towards that amount, father paid £100, myself £310, Amos £250, Irving £54, Arthur £50. Total £764 and we paid the remainder £236 during the following year, 1920.

POSTSCRIPT

When I was a small boy at a Sunday School Concert I was asked to sing a song, which I did, and the title of the song was, 'A Boy's Best Friend is his Mother'. How true it was in our experience. I always considered we had the best mother anyone could have.

S. Camplejohn

Sidney Camplejohn on his 90th birthday.

THE DARFIELD AREA AMENITY SOCIETY

The Darfield Area Amenity Society was founded in 1973 as a village civic society. In its 32 years of life, members have met regularly month by month and been involved in all manner of projects. These have involved environmental concerns; planning matters; social questions; the arts; village history; etc.

Whilst still being involved in all these and like matters, members have also now created the Maurice Dobson Museum & Heritage Centre in the village which involved the raising of £200,000 to restore the property at 2 Vicar Road, Darfield. Opening in 2000, the Museum has since raised over £50,000 in small grants for further capital work in the building; has amassed thousands of artefacts which help to tell the story of the village; and is now looking to create an interpretation centre in a nearby building. The Museum is run and staffed entirely by a group of willing volunteers.

Publication of this volume was made possible by a £1,500 grant from the South Yorkshire Foundation, to whom we are greatly indebted. It has been agreed that all profits from the sale of the book will be reserved to enable the publication of other books in the future by the Museum.

Geoffrey Hutchinson (Chairman),
The Maurice Dobson Museum & Heritage Centre,
2 Vicar Road,
Darfield,
Barnsley,
South Yorkshire.
S73 8LZ
November 2005